ÁF199000

Impressum
Verlag: BABADADA GmbH, Nedderfeld 112 , 22529 Hamburg
Geschäftsführer / Verlagsleitung: Harald Hof
Druck: Books on Demand GmbH, In de Tarpen 42, 22848 Norderstedt

Imprint
Publisher: BABADADA GmbH, Nedderfeld 112 , 22529 Hamburg, Germany
Managing Director / Publishing direction: Harald Hof
Print: Books on Demand GmbH, In de Tarpen 42, 22848 Norderstedt

school
escuela

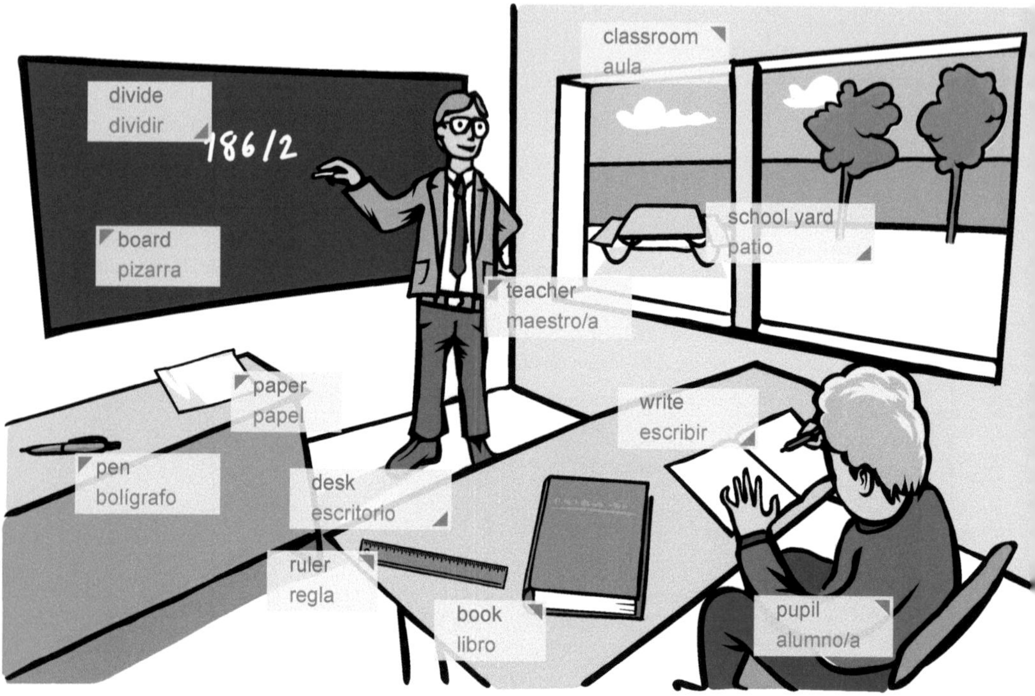
classroom
aula
divide
dividir
186/2
board
pizarra
school yard
patio
teacher
maestro/a
paper
papel
write
escribir
pen
bolígrafo
desk
escritorio
ruler
regla
book
libro
pupil
alumno/a

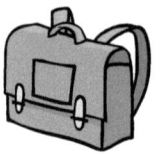

satchel

cartera

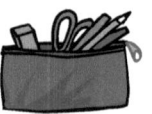

pencil case

caja de lápices

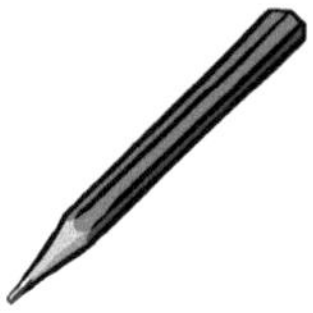

pencil

lápiz

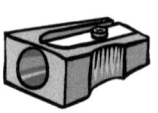

pencil sharpener

sacapuntas

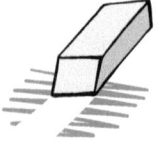

rubber

goma de borrar

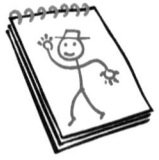

drawing pad

cuaderno de dibujo

drawing

dibujo

paintbrush

pincel

paint box

caja de pinturas

scissors

tijeras

glue

pegamento

exercise book

cuaderno de ejercicios

homework

deberes

number

número

add

sumar

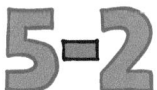

subtract

restar

multiply

multiplicar

calculate

calcular

letter

letra

alphabet

alfabeto

word

palabra

text

texto

read

leer

chalk

tiza

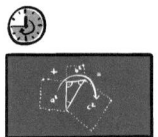

lesson

lección

register

cuaderno de notas

exam

examen

certificate

certificado

school uniform

uniforme escolar

education

educación

encyclopedia

enciclopedia

university

universidad

microscope

microscopio

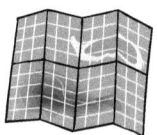

map

mapa

waste-paper basket

papelera

hotel
hotel

Grand

hostel
albergue

ROOMS

bureau de change
oficina de cambio de divisas

ECHANGE

car
coche

language
idioma

yes / no
sí / no

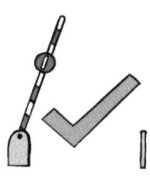

Okay
Vale

hello
hola

translator
traductor

Thank you
Gracias

how much is...?

¿cuánto es...?

I do not understand

No entiendo

problem

problema

Good evening!

¡Buenas tardes!

Good morning!

¡Buenos días!

Good night!

¡Buenas noches!

bye bye

adiós

direction

dirección

luggage

equipaje

bag

bolsa

backpack

mochila

guest

invitado

room

habitación

sleeping bag

saco de dormir

tent

tienda de campaña

travel - viaje

tourist information

información turística

beach

playa

credit card

tarjeta de crédito

breakfast

desayuno

lunch

almuerzo

dinner

cena

ticket

billete

lift

ascensor

stamp

sello

border

frontera

customs

aduana

embassy

embajada

visa

visa

passport

pasaporte

transport
transporte

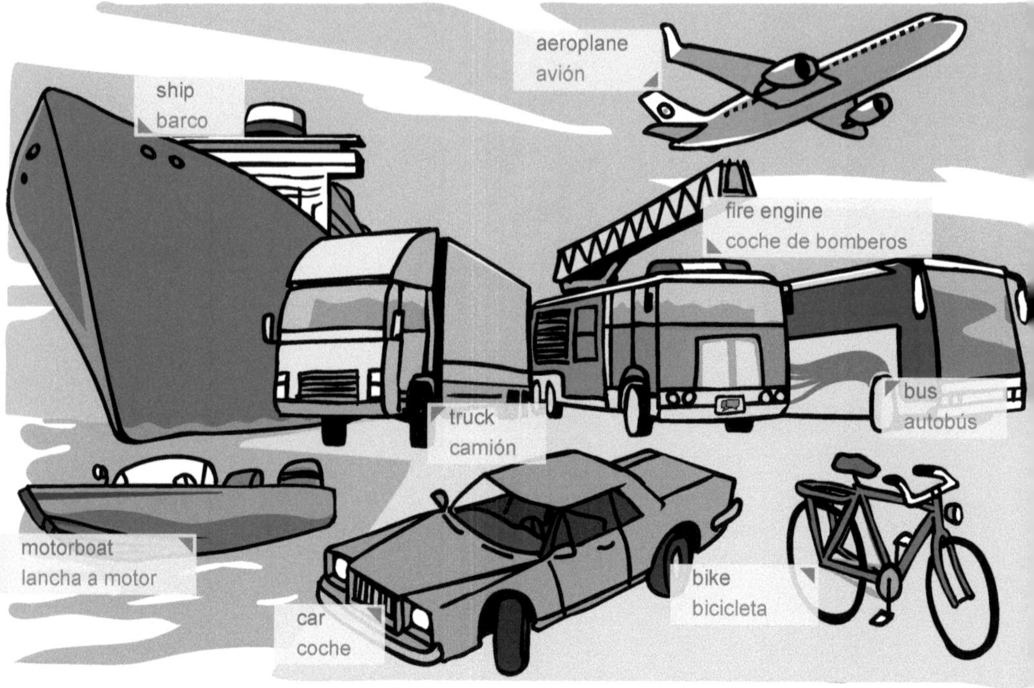
aeroplane
avión
ship
barco
fire engine
coche de bomberos
bus
autobús
truck
camión
motorboat
lancha a motor
bike
bicicleta
car
coche

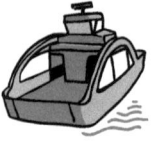

ferry
transbordador

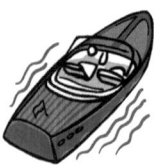

boat
barca

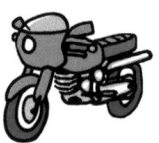

motorbike
moto

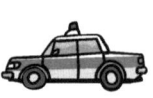

police car
coche de policía

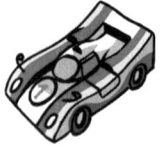

racing car
coche de carreras

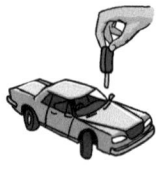

rental car
coche de alquiler

car sharing

préstamo de vehículos

breakdown truck

grúa

refuse truck

camión de la basura

motor

motor

fuel

gasolina

petrol station

gasolinera

traffic sign

señal de tráfico

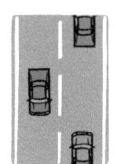

traffic

tráfico

traffic jam

atasco

car park

aparcamiento

train station

estación de tren

tracks

vías

train

tren

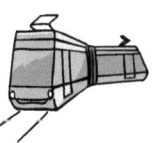

tram

tranvía

carriage

vagón

helicopter
helicóptero

airport
aeropuerto

tower
torre

passenger
pasajero

container
contenedor

carton
caja de cartón

cart
carretilla

basket
cesta

take off / land
despegar / aterrizar

city

ciudad

village
pueblo

city centre
centro de ciudad

house
casa

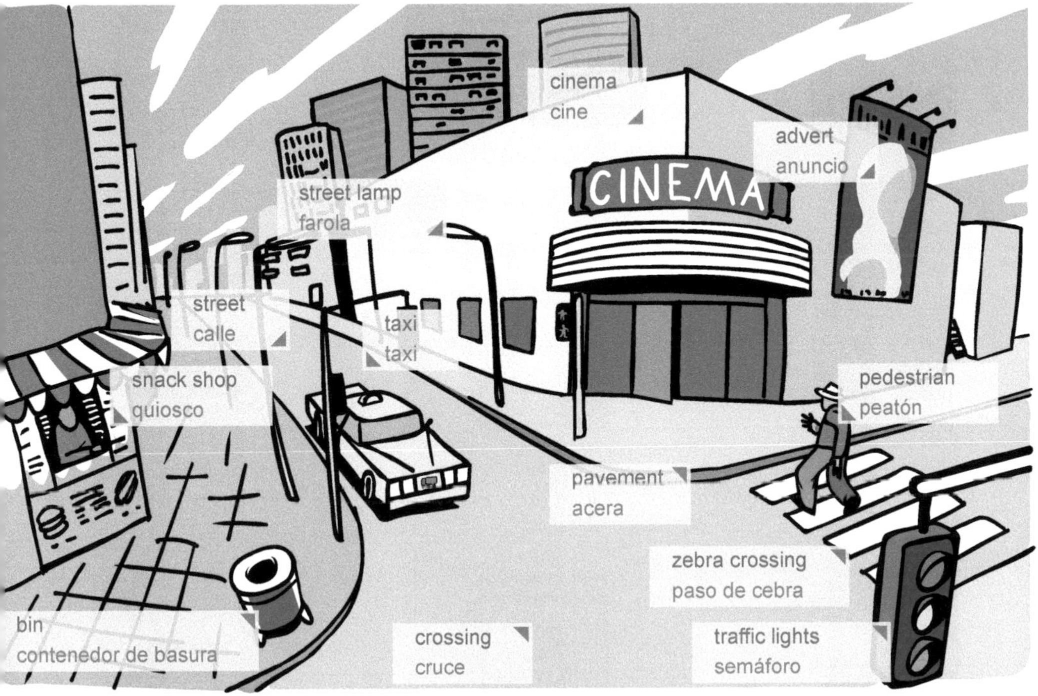

cinema
cine

advert
anuncio

street lamp
farola

CINEMA

street
calle

taxi
taxi

snack shop
quiosco

pedestrian
peatón

pavement
acera

zebra crossing
paso de cebra

bin
contenedor de basura

crossing
cruce

traffic lights
semáforo

hut

cabaña

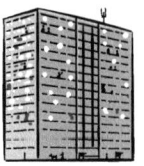

flat

apartamento

train station

estación de tren

town hall

ayuntamiento

museum

museo

school

escuela

university

universidad

bank

banco

hospital

hospital

hotel

hotel

pharmacy

farmacia

office

oficina

book shop

librería

shop

tienda

florist's

floristería

supermarket

supermercado

market

mercado

department store

grandes almacenes

fishmonger's

pescadería

shopping centre

centro comercial

harbour

puerto

city - ciudad

park

parque

bench

banco

bridge

puente

stairs

escaleras

underground

metro

tunnel

túnel

bus stop

parada de autobús

bar

bar

restaurant

restaurante

postbox

buzón

street sign

poste indicador

parking meter

parquímetro

zoo

zoo

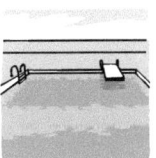

swimming pool

piscina

mosque

mezquita

farm
granja

pollution
contaminación

graveyard
cementerio

church
iglesia

playground
patio de juego

temple
templo

landscape

paisaje

signpost
señal

way
camino

meadow
prado

stone
piedra

tree
árbol

hiker
excursionista

river
río

grass
hierba

flower
flor

valley

valle

hill

colina

lake

lago

forest

bosque

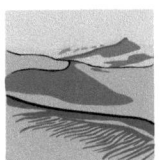

desert

desierto

volcano

volcán

castle

castillo

rainbow

arcoíris

mushroom

champiñón

palm tree

palmera

mosquito

mosquito

fly

mosca

ant

hormiga

bee

abeja

spider

araña

landscape - paisaje

beetle

escarabajo

frog

rana

squirrel

ardilla

hedgehog

erizo

hare

liebre

owl

lechuza

bird

pájaro

swan

cisne

boar

jabalí

deer

ciervo

moose

alce

dam

presa

wind turbine

turbina eólica

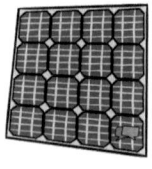

solar panel

panel solar

climate

clima

restaurant
restaurante

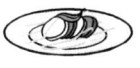

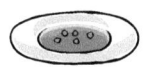

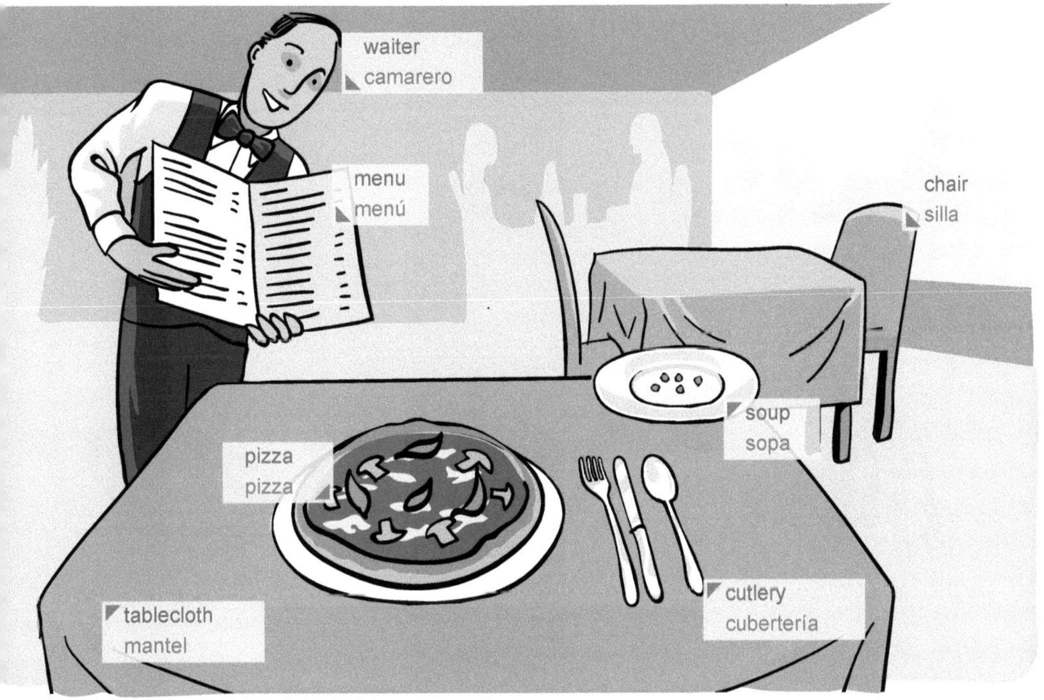
waiter
camarero
menu
menú
chair
silla
soup
sopa
pizza
pizza
cutlery
cubertería
tablecloth
mantel

starter
primer plato

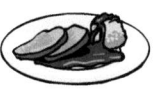

main course
plato principal

dessert
postre

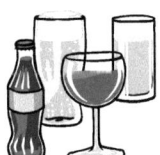

drinks
bebidas

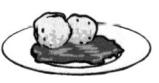

food
comida

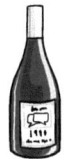

bottle
botella

fast food

comida rápida

street food

comida callejera

teapot

tetera

sugar bowl

azucarero

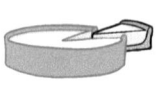

portion

porción

espresso machine

cafetera expreso

high chair

trona

bill

cuenta

tray

bandeja

knife

cuchillo

fork

tenedor

spoon

cuchara

teaspoon

cucharilla

serviette

servilleta

glass

vaso

restaurant - restaurante

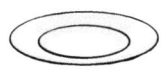

plate
plato

soup plate
plato hondo

saucer
platillo

sauce
salsa

salt pot
salero

pepper mill
molinillo de pimienta

vinegar
vinagre

oil
aceite

spices
especias

ketchup
ketchup

mustard
mostaza

mayonnaise
mayonesa

supermarket
supermercado

special offer
oferta especial
FOR
customer
cliente
dairy
lácteos
fruit
fruta
trolley
carro de la compra

BUTCHERS

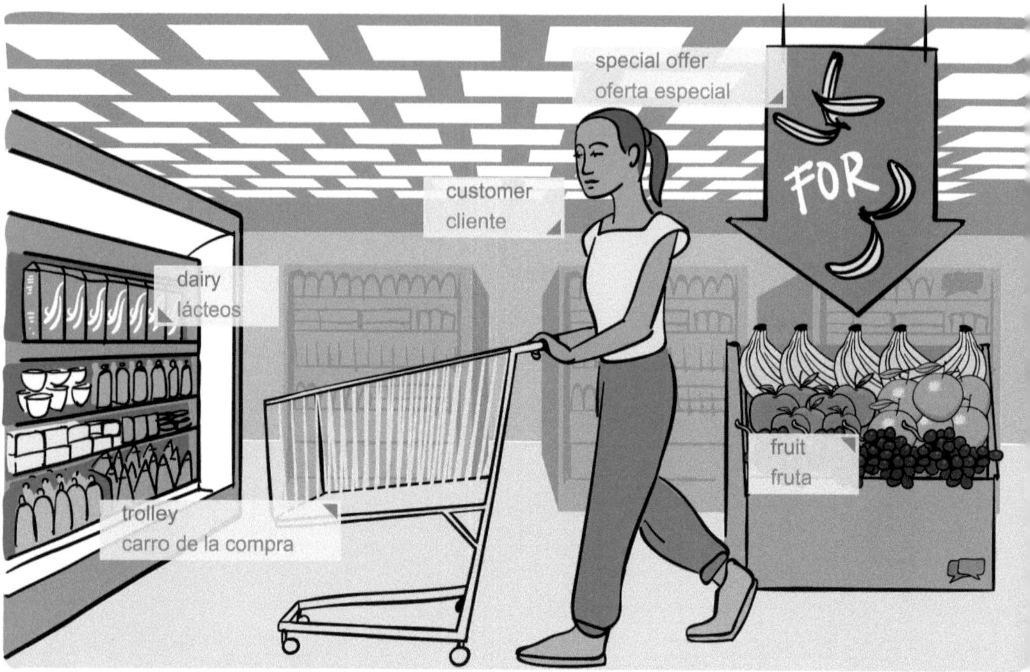

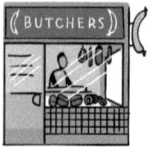

butcher´s

carnicería

BAKERY

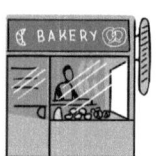

baker´s

panadería

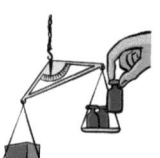

weigh

pesar

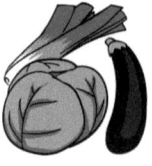

vegetables

verduras

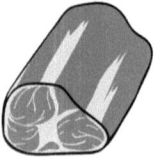

meat

carne

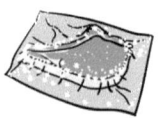

frozen food

alimentos congelados

cold meat

fiambres

tinned food

conservas

washing powder

detergente en polvo

sweets

dulces

household products

productos de uso doméstico

cleaning products

productos de limpieza

salesperson

vendedora

till

caja

cashier

cajero

shopping list

lista de la compra

opening hours

horario de atención al público

wallet

cartera

credit card

tarjeta de crédito

bag

bolsa

plastic bag

bolsa de plástico

drinks
bebidas

water

agua

juice

zumo

milk

leche

coke

cola

wine

vino

beer

cerveza

alcohol

alcohol

cocoa

cacao

tea

té

coffee

café

espresso

expreso

cappuccino

capuchino

banana

plátano

apple

manzana

orange

naranja

melon

melón

lemon

limón

carrot

zanahoria

garlic

ajo

bamboo

bambú

onion

cebolla

mushroom

champiñón

nuts

avellanas

noodles

fideos

spaghetti

espagueti

rice

arroz

salad

ensalada

chips

patatas fritas

fried potatoes

patatas fritas

pizza

pizza

hamburger

hamburguesa

sandwich

sándwich

cutlet

filete

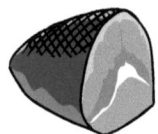

ham

jamón

salami

salami

sausage

salchicha

chicken

pollo

roast

asado

fish

pescado

food - comida

porridge oats

copos de avena

muesli

muesli

cornflakes

copos de maíz

flour

harina

croissant

cruasán

bread roll

panecillo

bread

pan

toast

tostada

biscuits

galletas

butter

mantequilla

curd

cuajada

cake

pastel

egg

huevo

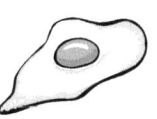

fried egg

huevo frito

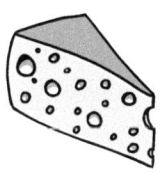

cheese

queso

ice cream

helado

sugar

azúcar

honey

miel

jam

mermelada

chocolate spread

crema de turrón

curry

curry

goat

cabra

cow

vaca

calf

ternero

pig

cerdo

piglet

cerdito

bull

toro

goose

ganso

duck

pato

chick

pollo

hen

gallina

cock

gallo

rat

rata

cat

gato

mouse

ratón

ox

buey

dog

perro

doghouse

perrera

garden hose

manguera

watering can

regadera

scythe

guadaña

plough

arado

sickle

hoz

hoe

azada

pitchfork

horca

axe

hacha

wheelbarrow

carretilla

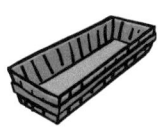

trough

abrevadero

milk can

lechera

sack

saco

fence

valla

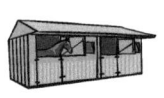

stable

establo

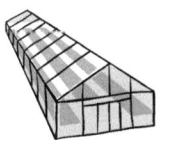

greenhouse

invernadero

soil

suelo

seed

semilla

fertilizer

fertilizador

combine harvester

cosechadora

harvest

cosechar

harvest

cosecha

yams

ñame

wheat

trigo

soy

soja

potato

patata

corn

maíz

rapeseed

semilla de colza

fruit tree

árbol frutal

cassava

mandioca

cereals

cereales

house

casa

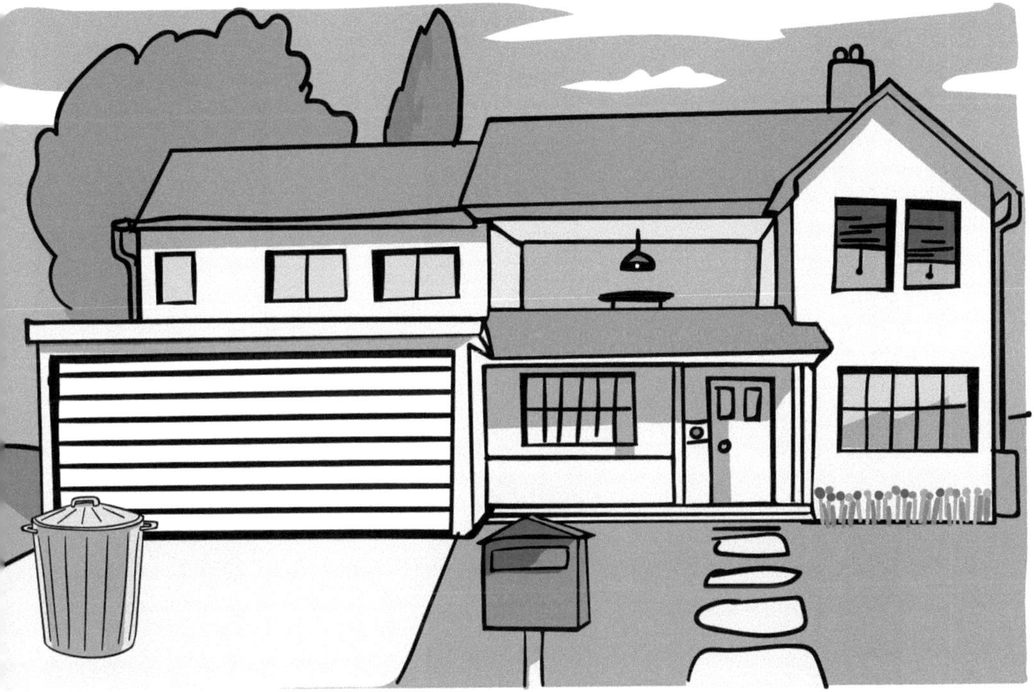

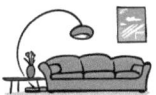

living room
....
sala

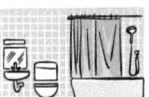

bathroom
....
cuarto de baño

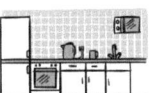

kitchen
....
cocina

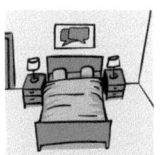

bedroom
....
dormitorio

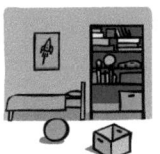

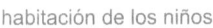

child's room
....
habitación de los niños

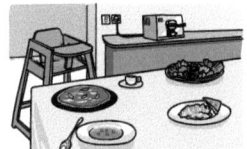

dining room
....
comedor

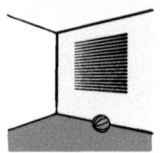

floor

suelo

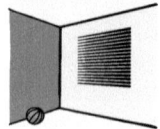

wall

pared

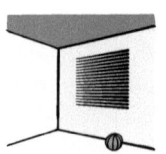

ceiling

techo

cellar

sótano

sauna

sauna

balcony

balcón

terrace

terraza

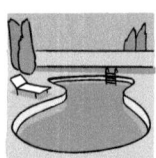

pool

piscina

lawn mower

cortacésped

sheet

sábana

bedspread

colcha

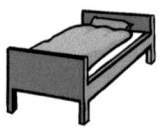

bed

cama

broom

escoba

bucket

balde

switch

interruptor

living room
sala

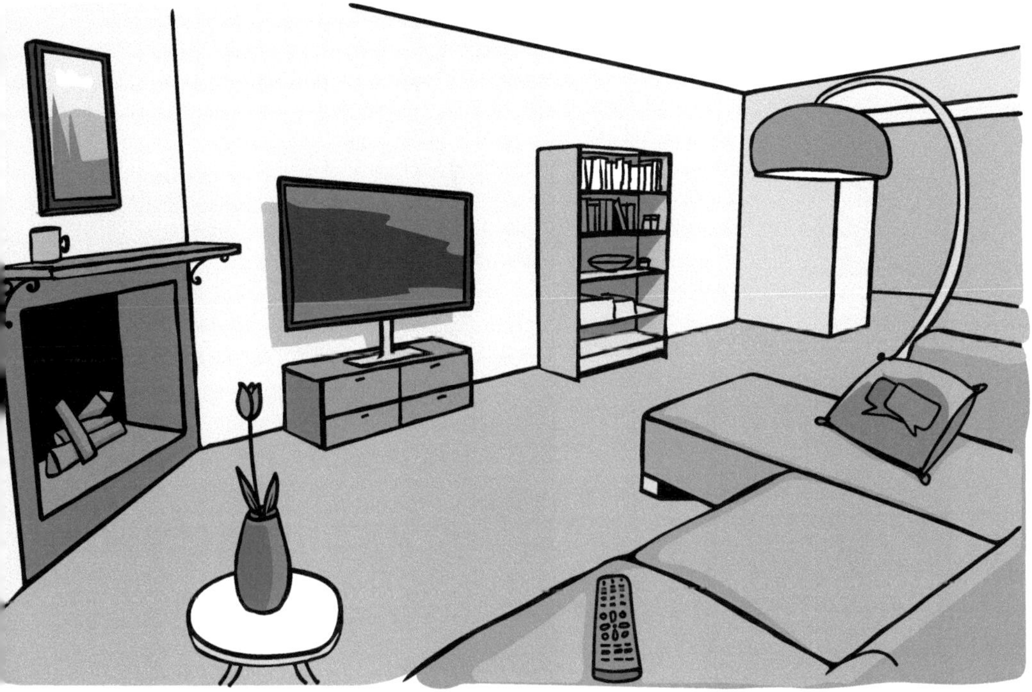

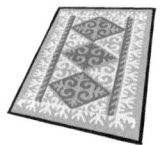

carpet
alfombra

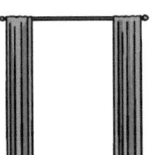

curtain
cortina

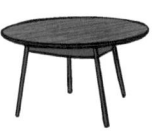

table
mesa

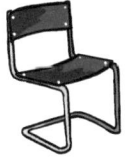

chair
silla

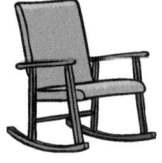

rocking chair
mecedora

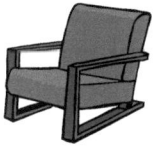

armchair
butaca

book
libro

blanket
manta

decoration
decoración

firewood
leña

film
película

hi-fi equipment
equipo de música

key
llave

newspaper
periódico

painting
pintura

poster
póster

radio
radio

notepad
cuaderno

hoover
aspiradora

cactus
cactus

candle
vela

kitchen
cocina

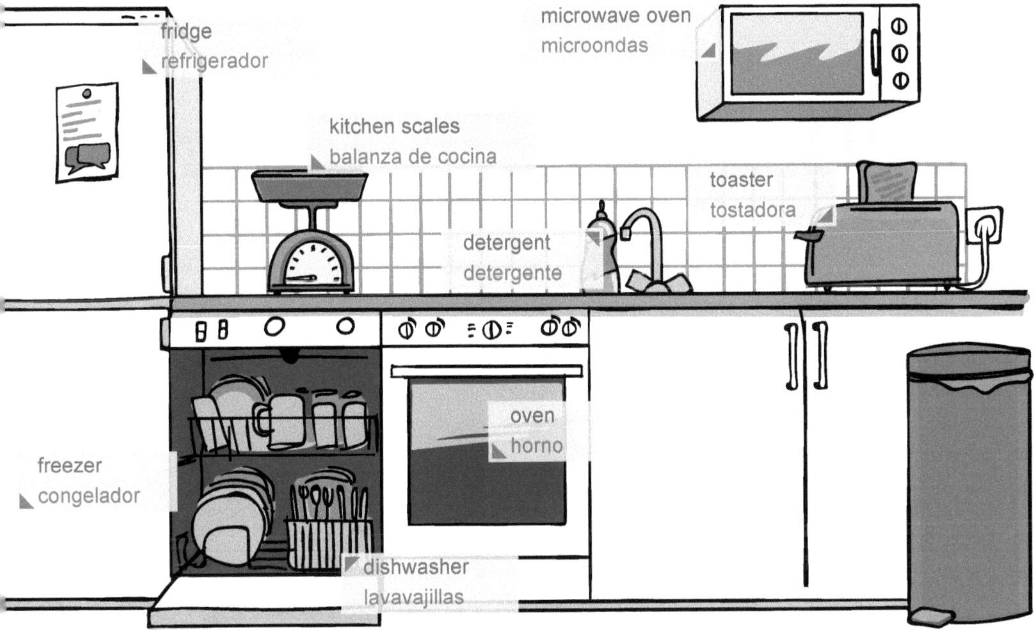

fridge
refrigerador
microwave oven
microondas
kitchen scales
balanza de cocina
toaster
tostadora
detergent
detergente
oven
horno
freezer
congelador
dishwasher
lavavajillas

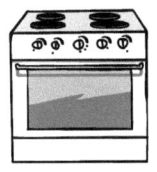

cooker

olla a presión

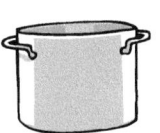

pot

olla

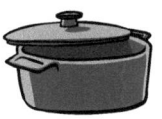

cast-iron pot

olla de hierro fundido

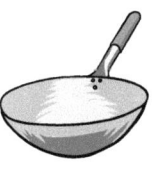

wok / kadai

wok / karahi

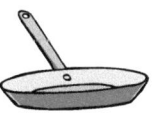

pan

cazuela

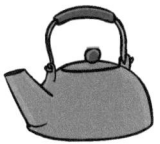

kettle

hervidor

steamer

vaporera

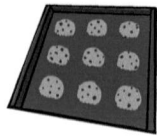

baking tray

chapa de horno

crockery

vajilla

mug

taza

bowl

tazón

chopsticks

palillos

ladle

cucharón

spatula

espumadera

whisk

batidor

strainer

colador

sieve

cedazo

grater

rallador

mortar

mortero

barbecue

barbacoa

open fire

hoguera

chopping board

tabla de picar

rolling pin

rodillo

corkscrew

sacacorchos

can

lata

can opener

abrelatas

pot holder

agarrador

sink

lavabo

brush

cepillo

sponge

esponja

blender

batidora

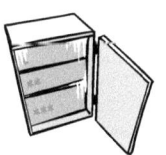

deep freezer

congelador

baby bottle

biberón

tap

grifo

kitchen - cocina

bathroom

cuarto de baño

heating
calefacción
towel
toalla
shower
ducha
shower curtain
cortina de la ducha
bubble bath
baño de espuma
bathtub
bañera
glass
vaso
washing machine
lavadora
tap
grifo
tiles
baldosas
potty
orinal
sink
lavabo

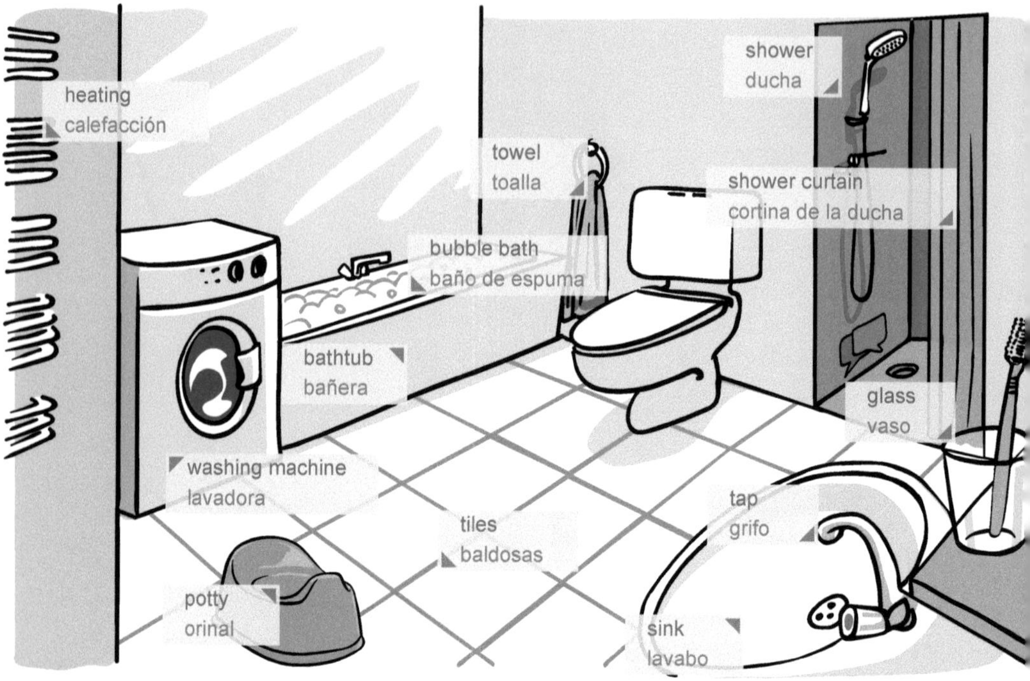

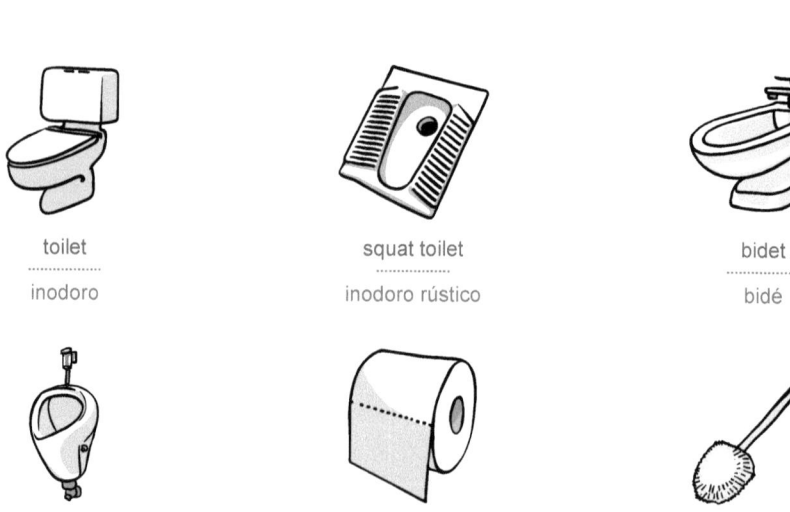

toilet

inodoro

squat toilet

inodoro rústico

bidet

bidé

urinal

urinario

toilet paper

papel higiénico

toilet brush

escobilla del váter

toothbrush

cepillo de dientes

toothpaste

pasta de dientes

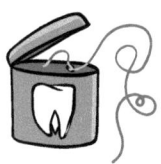

dental floss

hilo dental

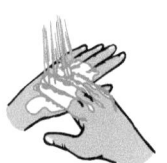

wash

lavar

handheld shower

ducha de mano

douche

ducha íntima

basin

pila

back brush

cepillo de espalda

soap

jabón

shower gel

gel de ducha

shampoo

champú

flannel

toallita

drain

desagüe

cream

crema

deodorant

desodorante

mirror

espejo

hand mirror

espejo de tocador

razor

maquinilla de afeitar

shaving foam

espuma de afeitar

aftershave

loción postafeitado

comb

peine

brush

cepillo

hair dryer

secador

hairspray

laca

makeup

maquillaje

lipstick

pintalabios

nail varnish

pintauñas

cotton wool

algodón

nail scissors

cortauñas

perfume

perfume

bathroom - cuarto de baño

washbag

estuche de viaje

stool

banqueta

weighing scale

balanza

bathrobe

albornoz

rubber gloves

guantes de goma

tampon

tampón

sanitary towel

compresa

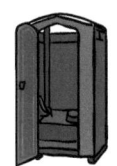

chemical toilet

inodoro químico

child's room

habitación de los niños

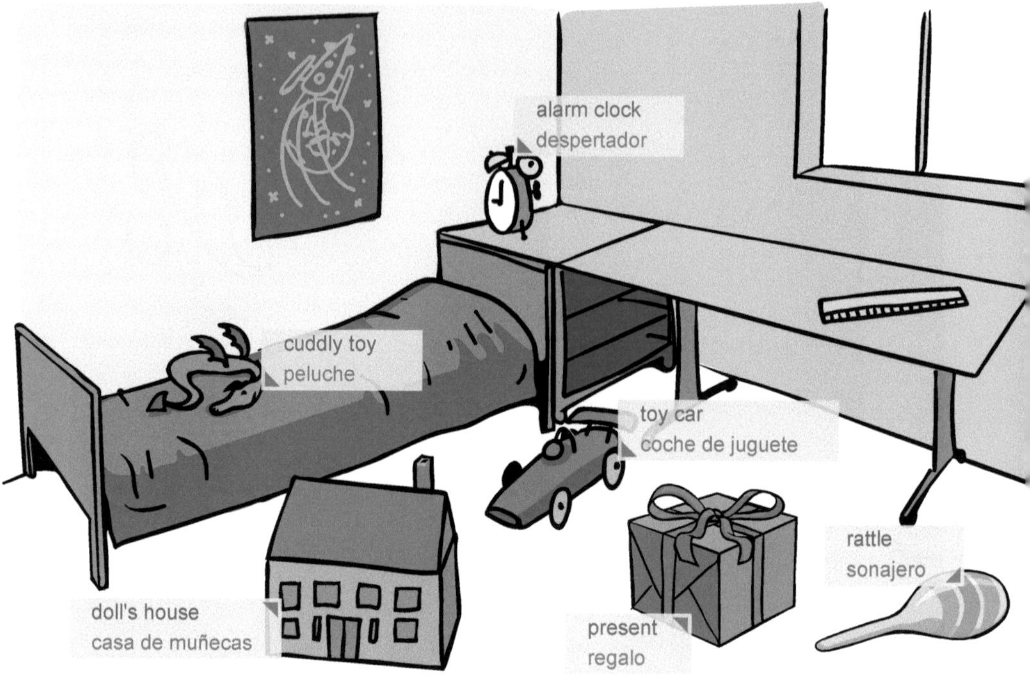

alarm clock
despertador
cuddly toy
peluche
toy car
coche de juguete
rattle
sonajero
doll's house
casa de muñecas
present
regalo

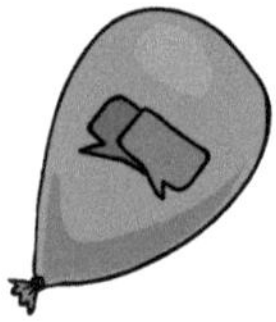

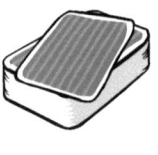

balloon

globo

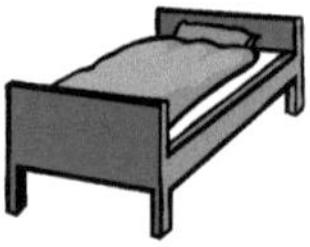

bed

cama

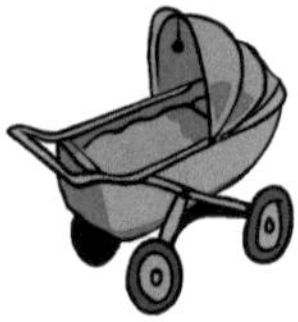

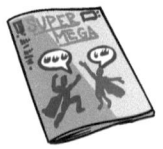

pram

coche de niño

deck of cards

naipes

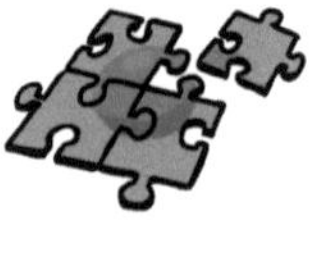

jigsaw

puzle

comic

tebeo

lego bricks

piezas de lego

building blocks

bloques de juguete

action figure

figura de acción

babygrow

bodi (de bebé)

frisbee

frisbee

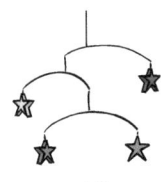

mobile

colgador móvil para bebés

board game

juego de mesa

dice

dados

model train set

circuito de tren eléctrico

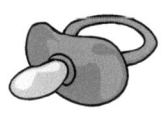

dummy

maniquí

party

fiesta

picture book

álbum de fotos

ball

pelota

doll

muñeca

play

jugar

sandpit

cajón de arena

swing

columpio

toys

juguetes

video game console

videoconsola

tricycle

triciclo

teddy bear

oso de peluche

wardrobe

guardarropa

clothing

ropa

socks

calcetines

stockings

medias

tights

leotardos

scarf
bufanda

belt
cinturón

umbrella
paraguas

t-shirt
camiseta

trainers
deportivas

boots
botas

slippers
zapatillas

sandals
....
sandalias

shoes
....
zapatos

rubber boots
....
botas de goma

underpants
....
slip

bra
....
sostén

vest
....
chaleco

body

bodi

trousers

pantalones

jeans

vaqueros

skirt

falda

blouse

blusa

shirt

camisa

pullover

jersey

hoodie

suéter

blazer

blazer

jacket

chaqueta

coat

abrigo

raincoat

gabardina

costume

traje

dress

vestido

wedding dress

vestido de novia

suit

traje

nightgown

camisón

pyjamas

pijama

sari

sari

headscarf

bandana

turban

turbante

burqa

burka

kaftan

caftán

abaya

abaya

swimsuit

traje de baño

trunks

bañador

shorts

pantalones cortos

tracksuit

chándal

apron

delantal

gloves

guantes

button

botón

glasses

gafas

bracelet

brazalete

necklace

collar

ring

anillo

earring

pendiente

cap

gorra

coat hanger

percha

hat

sombrero

tie

corbata

zip

cremallera

helmet

casco

braces

tirantes

school uniform

uniforme escolar

uniform

uniforme

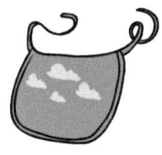

bib

babero

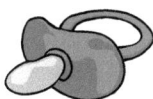

dummy

maniquí

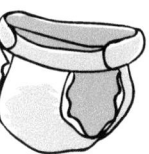

nappy

pañal

office
oficina

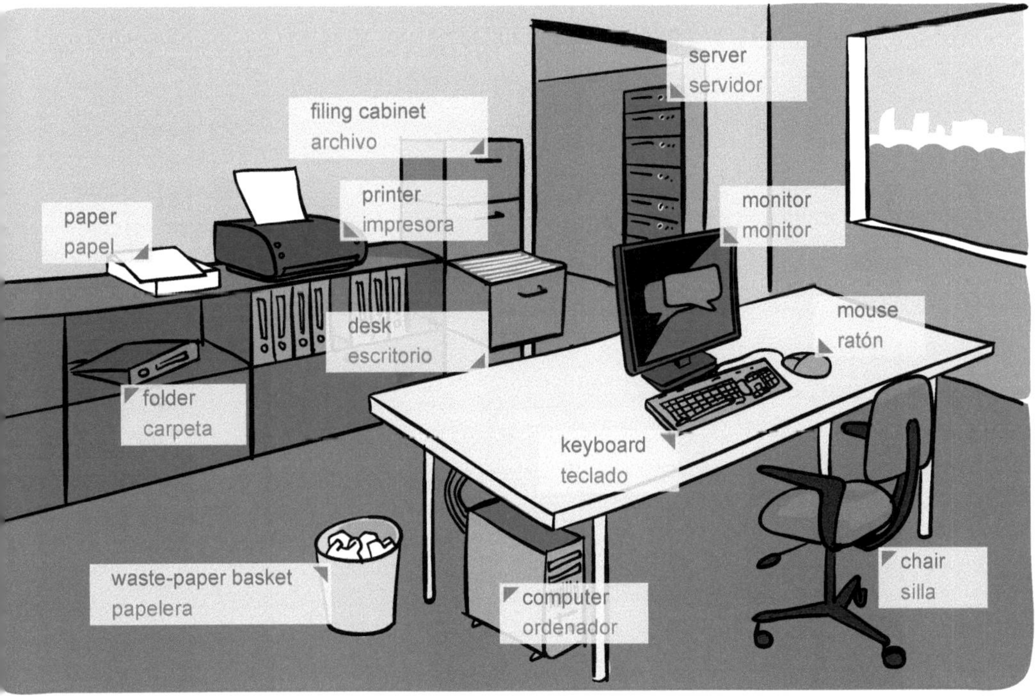

server
servidor
filing cabinet
archivo
printer
impresora
paper
papel
monitor
monitor
mouse
ratón
desk
escritorio
folder
carpeta
keyboard
teclado
chair
silla
waste-paper basket
papelera
computer
ordenador

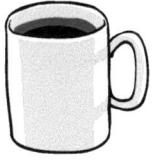

coffee mug

taza de café

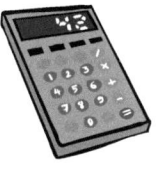

calculator

calculadora

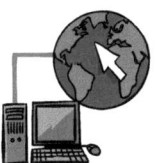

internet

internet

laptop

portátil

letter

carta

message

mensaje

mobile

móvil

network

red

photocopier

fotocopiadora

software

software

telephone

teléfono

plug socket

toma de corriente

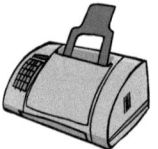

fax machine

fax

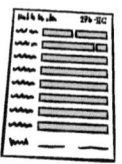

form

formulario

document

documento

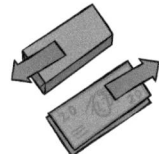

buy

comprar

pay

pagar

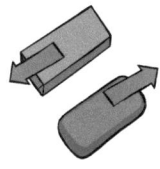

trade

comerciar

money

dinero

dollar

dólar

euro

euro

yen

yen

rouble

rublo

Swiss franc

franco suizo

renminbi yuan

renminbi yuan

rupee

rupia

cashpoint

cajero automático

bureau de change

oficina de cambio de divisas

gold

oro

silver

plata

oil

petróleo

energy

energía

price

precio

contract

contrato

tax

impuesto

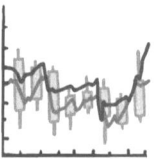

stock

acción

work

trabajar

employee

empleado

employer

empleador

factory

fábrica

shop

tienda

occupations
oficios

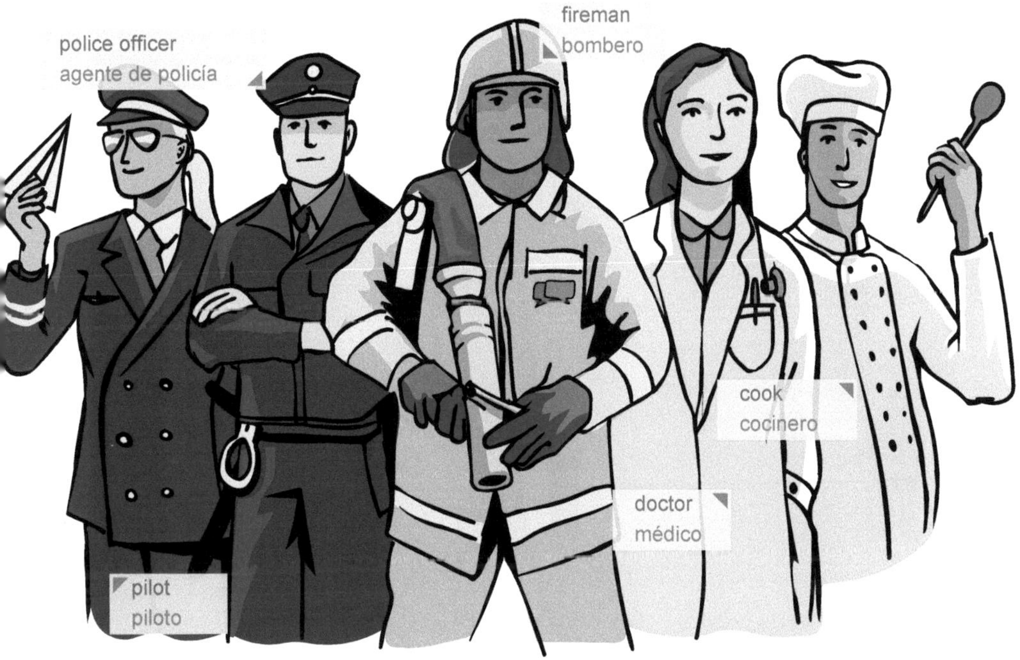
police officer
agente de policía
fireman
bombero
cook
cocinero
doctor
médico
pilot
piloto

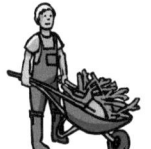

gardener
jardinero

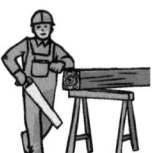

carpenter
carpintero

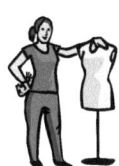

seamstress
costurera

judge
juez

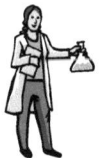

chemist
farmacéutico

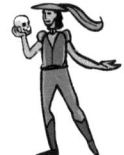

actor
actor

bus driver

conductor de autobús

taxi driver

taxista

fisherman

pescador

cleaning lady

señora de la limpieza

roofer

techador

waiter

camarero

hunter

cazador

painter

pintor

baker

panadero

electrician

electricista

builder

obrero

engineer

ingeniero

butcher

carnicero

plumber

fontanero

postman

cartero

soldier

soldado

architect

arquitecto

cashier

cajero

florist

florista

hairdresser

peluquero

conductor

revisor

mechanic

mecánico

captain

capitán

dentist

dentista

scientist

científico

rabbi

rabino

imam

imán

monk

monje

clergyman

sacerdote

tools
herramientas

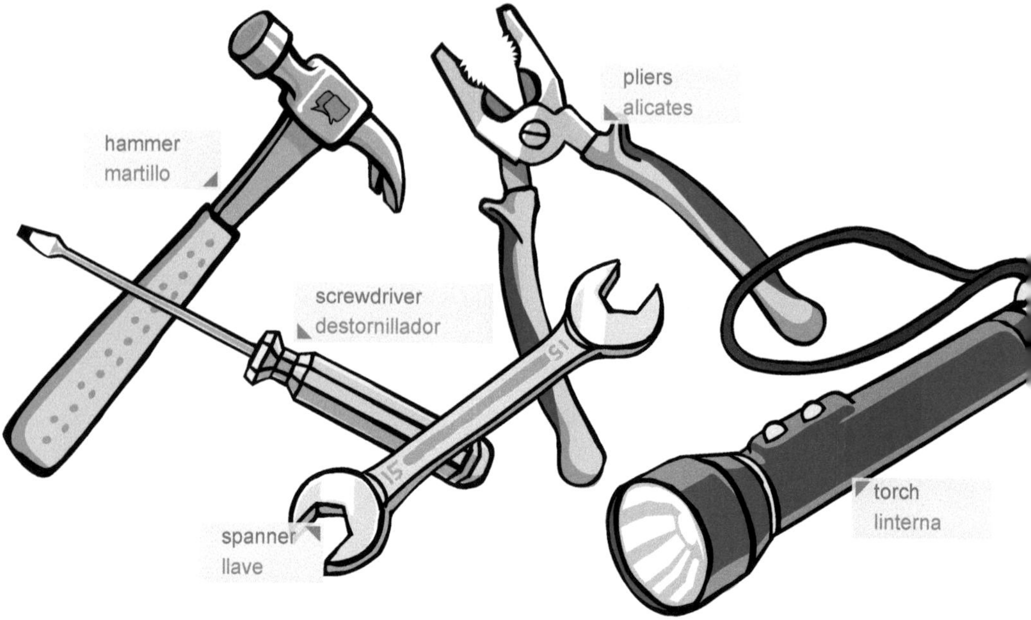

pliers
alicates
hammer
martillo
screwdriver
destornillador
torch
linterna
spanner
llave

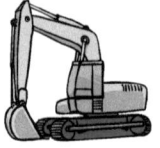

digger
excavadora

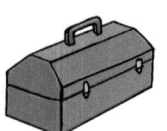

toolbox
caja de herramientas

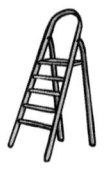

ladder
escalera de mano

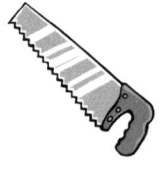

saw
sierra

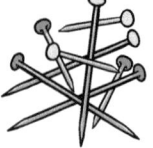

nails
clavos

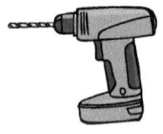

drill
taladro

repair

reparar

shovel

pala

Damn!

¡Maldita sea!

dustpan

recogedor

paint pot

bote de pintura

screws

tornillos

musical instruments

instrumentos musicales

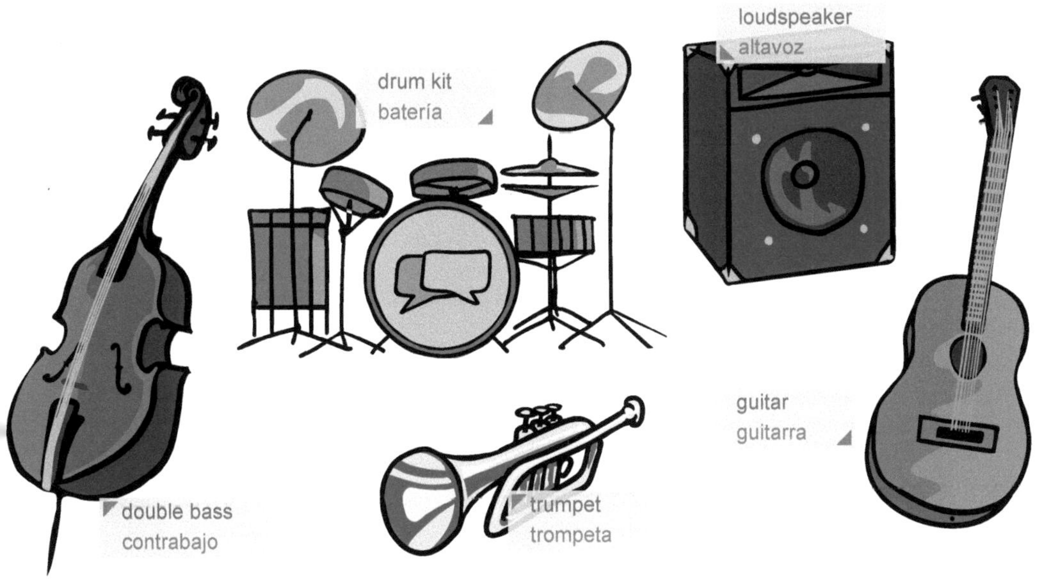

loudspeaker
altavoz

drum kit
batería

guitar
guitarra

double bass
contrabajo

trumpet
trompeta

piano

piano

violin

violín

bass

bajo

timpani

timbales

drums

tambor

keyboard

teclado

saxophone

saxofón

flute

flauta

microphone

micrófono

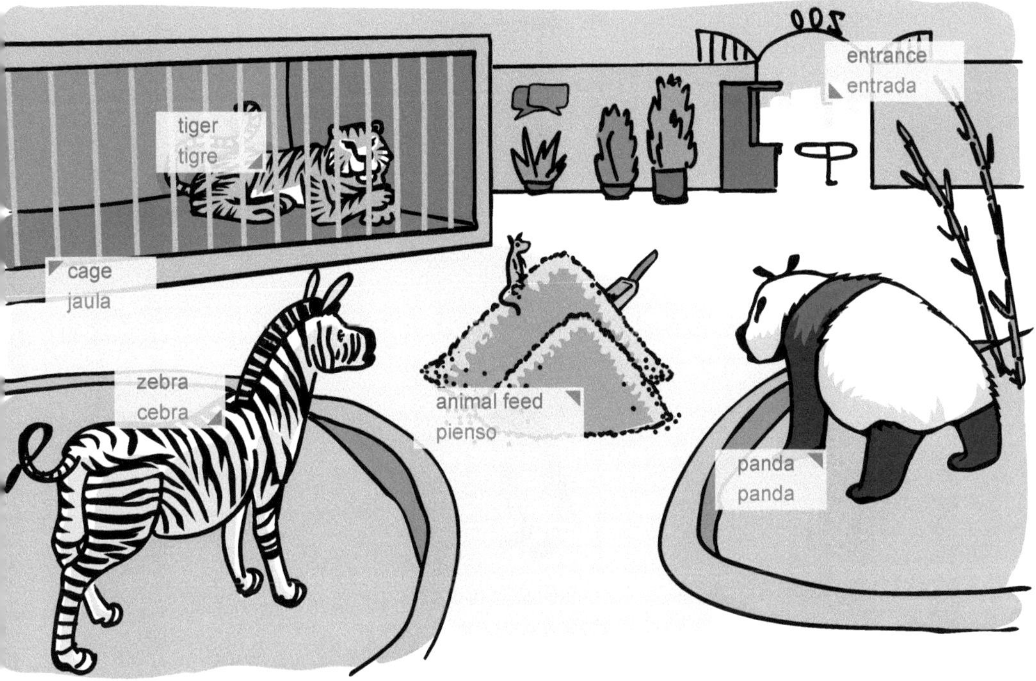

tiger
tigre

entrance
entrada

cage
jaula

zebra
cebra

animal feed
pienso

panda
panda

animals
animales

elephant
elefante

kangaroo
canguro

rhino
rinoceronte

gorilla
gorila

bear
oso

camel

camello

ostrich

avestruz

lion

león

monkey

mono

flamingo

flamingo

parrot

loro

polar bear

oso polar

penguin

pingüino

shark

tiburón

peacock

pavo real

snake

serpiente

crocodile

cocodrilo

zookeeper

guardián de zoológico

seal

foca

jaguar

jaguar

pony

poni

leopard

leopardo

hippo

hipopótamo

giraffe

jirafa

eagle

águila

boar

jabalí

fish

pescado

turtle

tortuga

walrus

morsa

fox

zorro

gazelle

gacela

American football
fútbol americano

cycling
ciclismo

tennis
tenis

basketball
baloncesto

swimming
natación

boxing
boxeo

ice hockey
hockey sobre hielo

football
fútbol

badminton
bádminton

athletics
atletismo

handball
balonmano

skiing
esquí

polo
polo

jump
saltar

laugh
reír

hug
abrazar

walk
caminar

sing
cantar

dream
soñar

pray
rezar

kiss
besar

write	draw	show
escribir	dibujar	mostrar

push	give	take
empujar	dar	tomar

have
tener

do
hacer

be
ser

stand
estar de pie

run
correr

pull
tirar

throw
tirar

fall
caer

lie
yacer

wait
esperar

carry
llevar

sit
estar sentado

get dressed
vestirse

sleep
dormir

wake up
despertar

look at

mirar

cry

llorar

stroke

acariciar

comb

peinar

talk

hablar

understand

entender

ask

preguntar

listen

escuchar

drink

beber

eat

comer

tidy up

ordenar

love

amar

cook

cocinar

drive

conducir

fly

volar

activities - actividades

sail

navegar

calculate

calcular

read

leer

learn

aprender

work

trabajar

marry

casarse

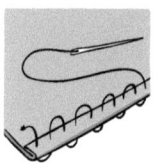

sew

coser

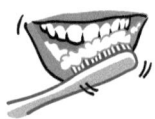

brush teeth

cepillarse los dientes

kill

matar

smoke

fumar

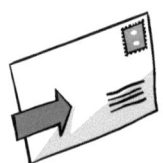

send

enviar

family
familia

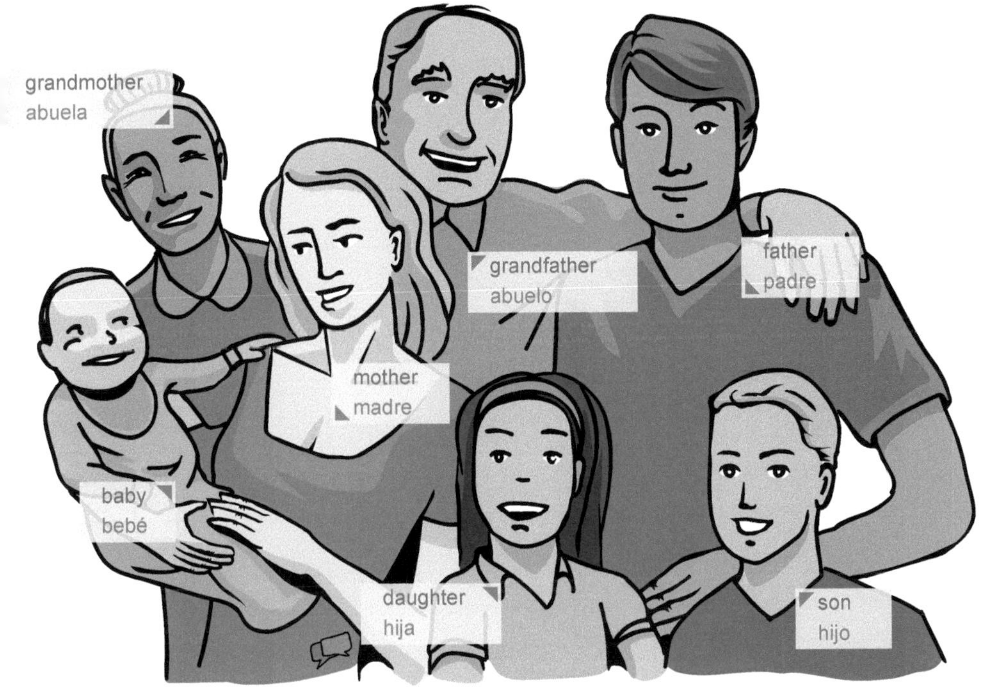
grandmother
abuela
grandfather
abuelo
father
padre
mother
madre
baby
bebé
daughter
hija
son
hijo

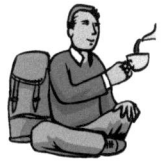

guest

invitado

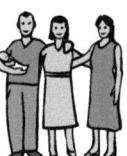

aunt

tía

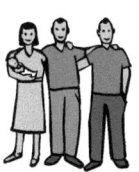

uncle

tío

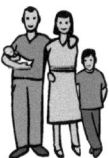

brother

hermano

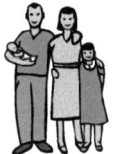

sister

hermana

body

cuerpo

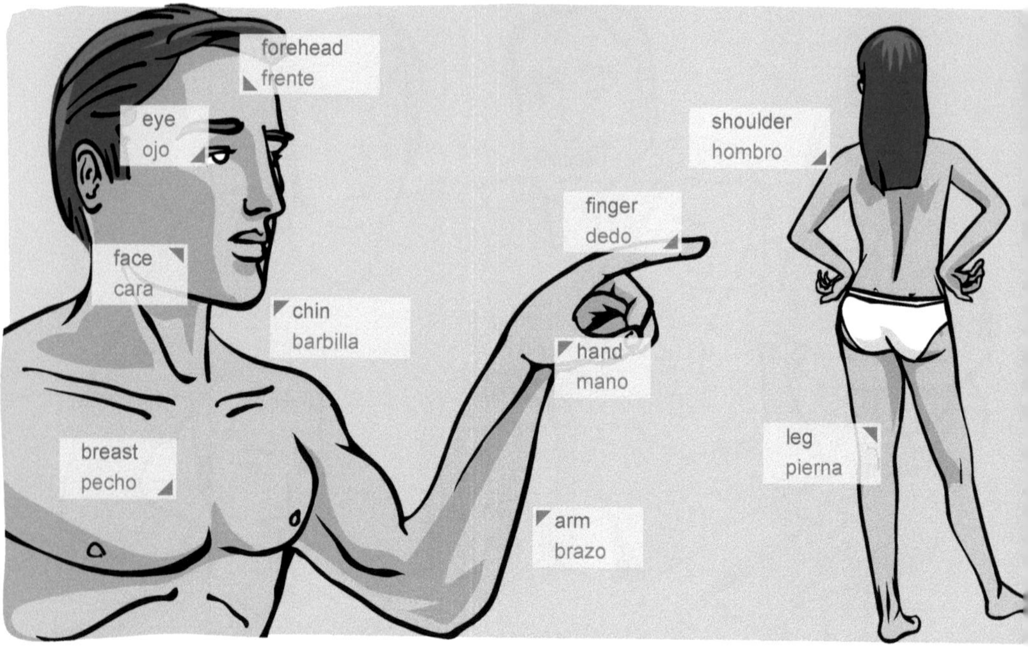

forehead
frente

eye
ojo

shoulder
hombro

finger
dedo

face
cara

chin
barbilla

hand
mano

breast
pecho

leg
pierna

arm
brazo

baby
bebé

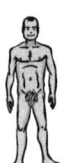

man
hombre

woman
mujer

girl
chica

boy
chico

head
cabeza

body - cuerpo

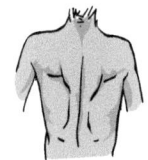	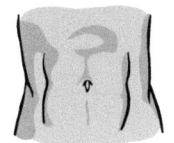	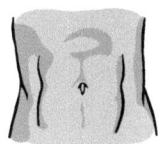
back	belly	belly button
espalda	vientre	ombligo
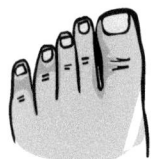	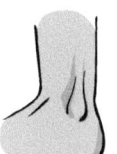	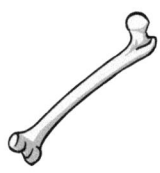
toe	heel	bone
dedo del pie	talón	hueso
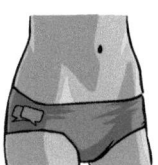	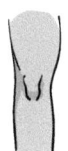	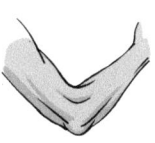
hip	knee	elbow
cadera	rodilla	codo
	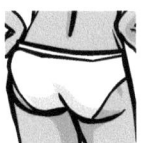	
nose	bottom	skin
nariz	trasero	piel
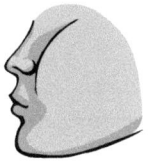	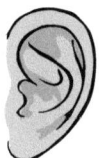	
cheek	ear	lip
mejilla	oído	labio

mouth

boca

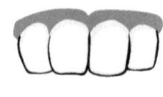

tooth

diente

tongue

lengua

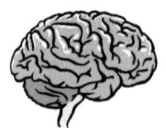

brain

cerebro

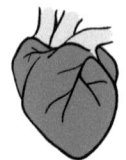

heart

corazón

muscle

músculo

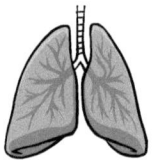

lung

pulmón

liver

hígado

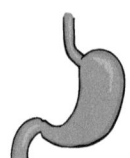

stomach

estómago

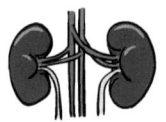

kidneys

riñones

sex

sexo

condom

condón

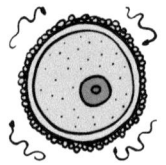

ovum

ovario

semen

semen

pregnancy

embarazo

body - cuerpo

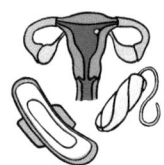

menstruation

menstruación

vagina

vagina

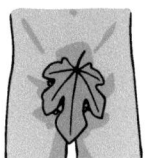

penis

pene

eyebrow

ceja

hair

pelo

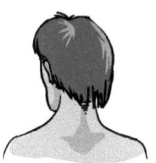

neck

cuello

hospital
hospital

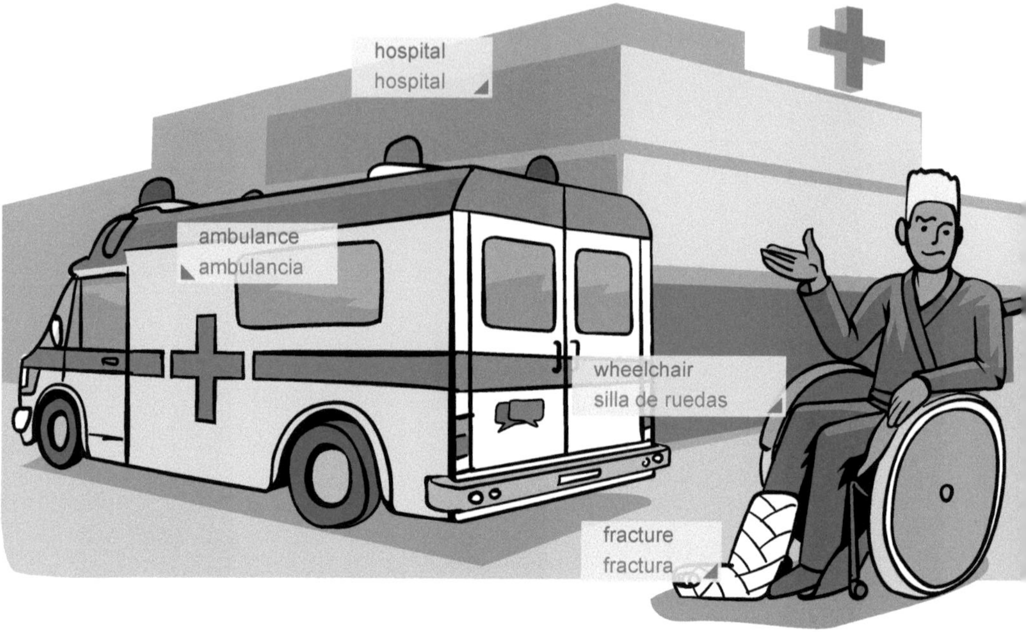

hospital
hospital
ambulance
ambulancia
wheelchair
silla de ruedas
fracture
fractura

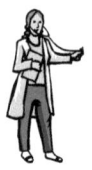

doctor

médico

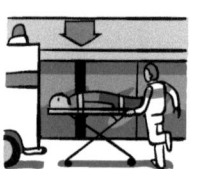

emergency room

sala de urgencias

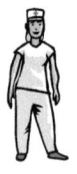

nurse

enfermera

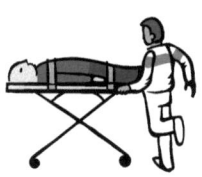

emergency

urgencia

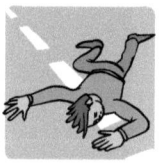

unconscious

inconsciente

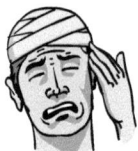

pain

dolor

injury

lesión

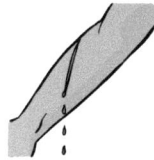
bleeding

hemorragia

heart attack

infarto

stroke

ictus

allergy

alergia

cough

tos

fever

fiebre

flu

gripe

diarrhoea

diarrea

headache

dolor de cabeza

cancer

cáncer

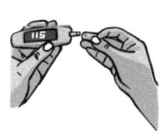
diabetes

diabetes

surgeon

cirujano

scalpel

bisturí

operation

operación

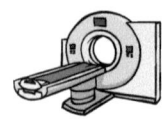

CT

TAC

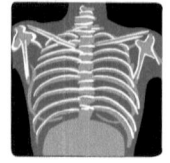

x-ray

rayos x

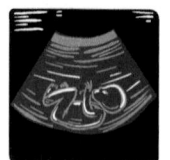

ultrasound

ultrasonido

face mask

mascarilla

disease

enfermedad

waiting room

sala de espera

crutch

muleta

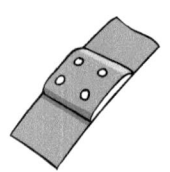

plaster

tirita

bandage

venda

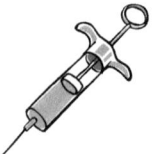

injection

inyección

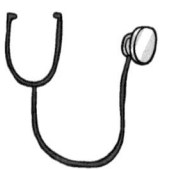

stethoscope

estetoscopio

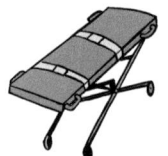

stretcher

camilla

clinical thermometer

termómetro

birth

nacimiento

overweight

sobrepeso

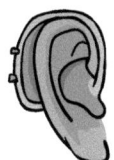

hearing aid

audífono

disinfectant

desinfectante

infection

infección

virus

virus

HIV / AIDS

VIH / SIDA

medicine

medicina

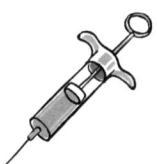

vaccination

vacunación

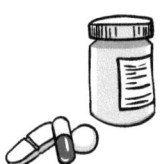

tablets

tabletas

pill

pastilla

emergency call

llamada de urgencia

blood pressure monitor

tensiómetro

ill / healthy

enfermo / sano

Help!  alarm  assault

¡Socorro! alarma asalto

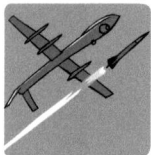  

attack danger emergency exit

ataque peligro salida de emergencia

Fire!  fire extinguisher  accident

¡Fuego! extintor de incendios accidente

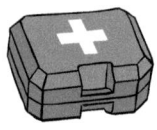  

first-aid kit SOS police

botiquín de primeros auxilios SOS policía

Europe

Europa

North America

Norteamérica

South America

Sudamérica

Africa

África

Asia

Asia

Australia

Australia

Atlantic

Atlántico

Pacific

Pacífico

Indian Ocean

Océano Índico

Antarctic Ocean

Océano Antártico

Arctic Ocean

Océano Ártico

North Pole

polo norte

South Pole
polo sur

Antarctica
Antártida

Earth
tierra

land
tierra

sea
mar

island
isla

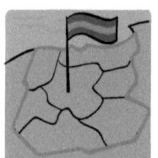

nation
nación

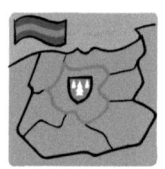

state
estado

clock face

esfera

hour hand

manecilla de las horas

minute hand

minutero

second hand

segundero

What time is it?

¿Qué hora es?

day

día

time

tiempo

now

ahora

digital watch

reloj digital

minute

minuto

hour

hora

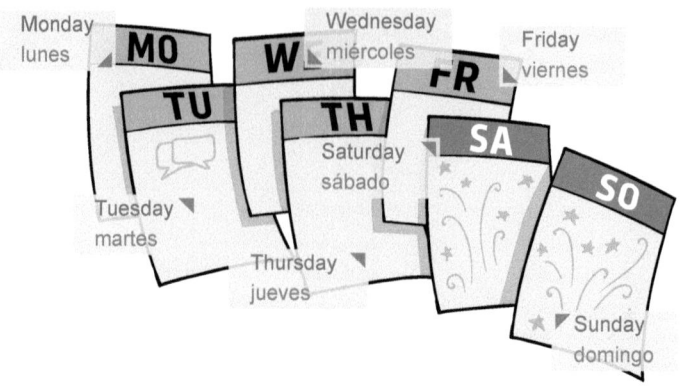

Monday — lunes
Wednesday — miércoles
Friday — viernes
Tuesday — martes
Saturday — sábado
Thursday — jueves
Sunday — domingo

yesterday

ayer

today

hoy

tomorrow

mañana

morning

mañana

noon

mediodía

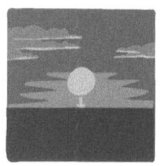

evening

tarde

business days

días laborables

weekend

fin de semana

year
año

rain
lluvia
snow
nieve
wind
viento
spring
primavera
autumn
otoño
summer
verano
winter
invierno

4.APRIL 11°
5.APRIL 4°
6.APRIL 13°
7.APRIL 8°
8.APRIL 10°

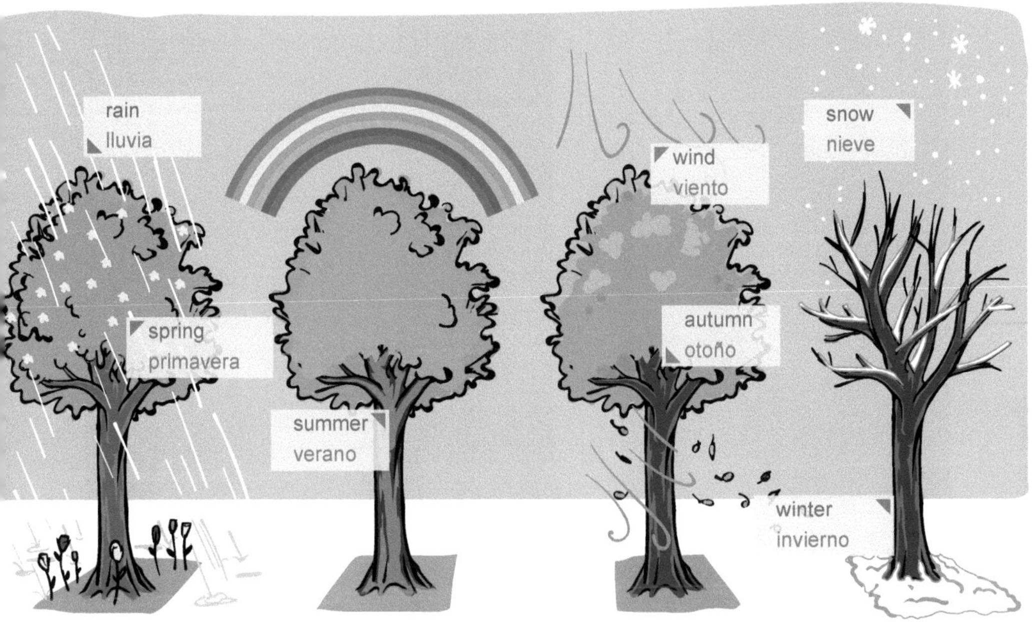

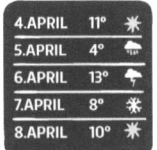

weather forecast
pronóstico del tiempo

F
C
120
90
60
30
0
-30
40
30
20
10
0
-10
-20

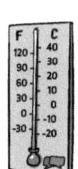

thermometer
termómetro

sunshine
sol

cloud
nube

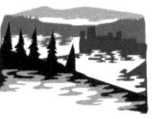

fog
niebla

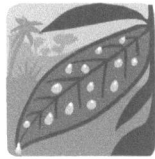

humidity
humedad

lightning

rayo

thunder

trueno

storm

tormenta

hail

granizo

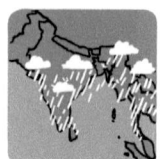

monsoon

monzón

flood

inundación

ice

hielo

January

enero

February

febrero

March

marzo

April

abril

May

mayo

June

junio

July

julio

August

agosto

September
....
septiembre

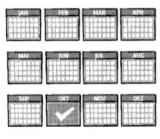

October
....
octubre

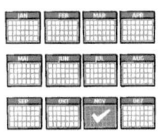

November
....
noviembre

December
....
diciembre

circle
....
círculo

square
....
cuadrado

rectangle
....
rectángulo

triangle
....
triángulo

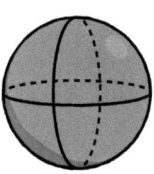

sphere
....
esfera

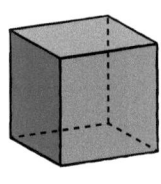

cube
....
cubo

colores

white
....
blanco

yellow
....
amarillo

orange
....
anaranjado

pink
....
rosa

red
....
rojo

purple
....
morado

blue
....
azul

green
....
verde

brown
....
marrón

grey
....
gris

black
....
negro

a lot / a little

mucho / poco

angry / calm

enojado / tranquilo

beautiful / ugly

bonito / feo

beginning / end

principio / fin

big / small

grande / pequeño

bright / dark

claro / oscuro

brother / sister

hermano / hermana

clean / dirty

limpio / sucio

complete / incomplete

completo / incompleto

day / night

día / noche

dead / alive

muerto / vivo

wide / narrow

ancho / estrecho

edible / inedible

comestible / no comestible

evil / kind

malo / amable

excited / bored

entusiasmado / aburrido

fat / thin

gordo / delgado

first / last

primero / último

friend / enemy

amigo / enemigo

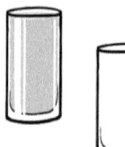

full / empty

lleno / vacío

hard / soft

duro / blando

heavy / light

pesado / ligero

hunger / thirst

hambre / sed

ill / healthy

enfermo / sano

illegal / legal

ilegal / legal

intelligent / stupid

inteligente / tonto

left / right

izquierda / derecha

near / far

cerca / lejos

new / used

nuevo / usado

nothing / something

nada / algo

old / young

viejo / joven

on / off

encendido / apagado

open / closed

abierto / cerrado

quiet / loud

silencioso / ruidoso

rich / poor

rico / pobre

right / wrong

correcto / incorrecto

rough / smooth

áspero / suave

sad / happy

triste / contento

short / long

corto / largo

slow / fast

lento / rápido

wet / dry

húmedo / seco

warm / cool

cálido / frío

war / peace

guerra / paz

numbers

números

0

zero

cero

1

one

uno

2

two

dos

3

three

tres

4

four

cuatro

5

five

cinco

6

six

seis

7

seven

siete

8

eight

ocho

9

nine

nueve

10

ten

diez

11

eleven

once

12

twelve

doce

13

thirteen

trece

14

fourteen

catorce

15

fifteen

quince

16

sixteen

dieciséis

17

seventeen

diecisiete

18

eighteen

dieciocho

19

nineteen

diecinueve

20

twenty

veinte

100

hundred

cien

1.000

thousand

mil

1.000.000

million

millón

English
inglés

American English
inglés americano

Chinese Mandarin
chino mandarín

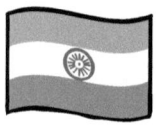

Hindi
hindi

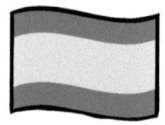

Spanish
español

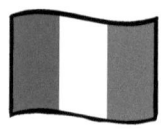

French
francés

Arabic
árabe

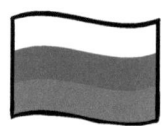

Russian
ruso

Portuguese
portugués

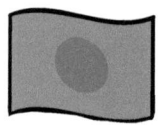

Bengali
bengalí

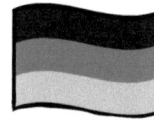

German
alemán

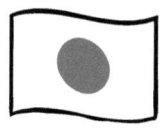

Japanese
japonés

I
yo

you
tú

he / she / it
él / ella / ello

we
nosotros/as

you
vosotros/as

they
ellos/as

who?
¿quién?

what?
¿qué?

how?
¿cómo?

where?
¿dónde?

when?
¿cuándo?

name
nombre

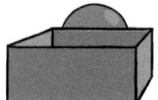

behind

detrás

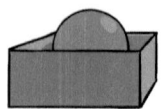

in

en

in front of

delante de

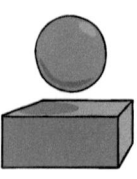

over

por encima de

on

sobre

under

debajo de

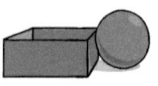

beside

junto a

between

entre

place

lugar